I0086092

Published by Emma Gibbens

First published in 2024 in Perth, Australia

Edited by Jenny Magee
www.jennymagee.com

Designed by Nathan Maddigan
www.nathanmaddigan.com

Typeset and printed in Australia by Self Titled Studios
www.selftitledstudios.com

All artwork by Rhys Paddick
@the_wholesome_yamatji

A catalogue record for this work is available from the National Library of Australia.

National Library of Australia Cataloguing-in-Publication data:

Creator:	Gibbens, Emma.
Title:	Anatomy of Conversation / Emma Gibbens.
ISBN:	978-0-6454857-2-1 (paperback)
	978-0-6454857-3-8 (ebook)
Subjects:	Sociology.
	Soft skills and dealing with other people.

First Edition

Contents

ANATOMY OF CONVERSATION

EMMA GIBBENS

Acknowledging Country

I'm Emma and I come from cold, dark places. Minnesota and Alaska, to be specific. My family is a long line of migrants: my grandma Marge migrated from Finland as a girl, my parents drove up to Alaska, and now I have moved to Australia. When I consider the relationship between Indigenous peoples and migrants, I'm pretty firmly in the migrant camp.

I am humbled by all I learn from traditional culture. Connection and conversation seem to be central to this way of knowing. I am honoured to carry on a practice that has been around for tens of thousands of years.

I hope to honour my ancestors by contributing in a meaningful way, to continue to participate in and positively shape our shared culture. I'd like to pay respects to the peoples, cultures, histories and traditional custodians of the lands I grew up on, the Anishinaabeg, Ojibwe, and Chippewa nations, and the place I call home today, Whadjuk Noongar Boodjar.

All our elders, past and present, carry wisdom that I hope to live up to and pass on.

Introduction

Hey you.

I wrote this book for you. Well, for all of us really.

We communicate all the time, yet it seems that sharing words is driving us further apart.

Discussion has halted. Become stagnant or at odds. A conversation between two people or within a team or family can become a sparring match or a meaningless void. We are talking *at* each other, not *with* each other. We leave wanting more or so hurt that we refuse to engage again. Many voices have become too loud, shouting, not caring if anyone is listening. Some of us have confused the intent of communication and believe speaking without thinking is the same as speaking the truth. Are transactional passings of phrase the food that feeds true connection?

We underestimate and undervalue the power of conversation. It is more than using our mouths to make sounds. Rather than stumbling haphazardly into these conversations, we can think it through and plan. With a bit of preparation, you can more easily navigate the complexity mid-conversation.

We can't improve what we don't understand. We need to examine conversations, turn each element over and tinker with how they fit together for us individually and for our specific situations. By understanding the structure and how the pieces interact we gain confidence to navigate the tricky bits.

Courageous conversations enable meaningful connection, where we get to see deeper, different and truer sides of ourselves and each other.

When we overcome fear and step forth courageously into more expansive conversations, we find greater connection. This is where we sort through the mess and find common ground. We harmonise and heal. These conversations feel precarious but offer the far greater reward of meaningful connection.

On an individual level, connection nurtures us. It restores our faith and hope in humanity by expanding our understanding and empathy.

At a community or system level, connection creates a network we can participate in, spinning a web of safety for us all.

Our ancestors gathered around the fire to discuss, resolve and dream. Around the fire, we whoop, laugh and sing. We tell stories to teach, share and inspire.

We explore challenges openly and without manipulation. Around the fire, every voice is heard as we speak new possibilities into being. The verbal seeds are planted, our actions are influenced, and ways of being are changed.

We grow our connections through the ancient practice of conversation. Let us all become fluent in the Anatomy of Conversation so that we can navigate all the complexity that is to come, together.

Conversations change the world

If I could wave a magic wand and wish for anything, I would wish for the power to facilitate any conversation. To know how to hold difficult ones, accelerate impactful ones and invite in those who resist connection.

Conversations are magic. They change the world by turning individuals into community, creating something new and available only in that moment. This is the definition of presence. This exchange of ideas and feelings creates something greater than the sum of its parts.

Conversations connect us. We build connection by sharing stories and experiences, creating understanding and empathy. Greater connection builds stronger communities of stronger people, which empower us individually and collectively to live better.

These conversations are expansive, fulfilling and revealing. Full of newness and discovery and a deep resonance of our common threads.

The power of conversation is universally human. We have them in our professional and personal lives, with loved ones, with people we disagree with and with people we don't know. Having more meaningful conversations is beneficial for everyone.

Conversation is free and accessible to everyone by whatever means available, using language or otherwise. It is an innately human practice.

When challenges inevitably happen, conversations help assess the situation and determine what needs to be done. That is how we become more adaptable and find strength among the chaos. Conversations build resilience.

Conversations are complex. Each requires a bit of energy to navigate appropriately. They are organic things of beauty, changing at the turn of a word, tone or posture.

With any complex conversation, it's the *process* that matters. We build the solutions together.

Conversations are a container to explore our shared humanity.

Conversations help us truly see and understand each other.

Conversations encourage us to embrace difference.

Conversations move us forward.

Conversations change our world.

About your author

For me, this work started in 2008 when I was working to elect Barack Obama and Al Franken. Calling voters in Northern Minnesota to talk about electing a black man and a comedian showed me the power of conversation to open people's hearts and move beyond bias.

From there, I worked on political and advocacy campaigns for over 15 years, specialising in grassroots movements. We built people machines of volunteers working together having conversations with their neighbours and community towards a common purpose.

Since then, I have stepped away from recruitment and persuasion conversations into culture conversations, facilitating reflection, awareness and ultimately participation in our shared culture.

I have more than 10,000 hours of experience in wonderful, awkward, enlightening, silly, sticky and tricky conversations. This references Malcolm Gladwell's idea that we become skilled through practice and 10,000 hours lead us to expertise.[1]

The power of conversations translates across continents and cultures. We gather together and discuss our honest expressions. This enables us to go deeper, find our common ground, and move forward.

Even as an expert in conversation and facilitation craft, I am still learning. New scenarios with new people in new places means my conversation practice is shaped by the changing context. I am learning right alongside you.

This book could have been written for specific people in specific roles having specific conversations. Perhaps for not-for-profit leaders who want to further their cause, or team managers who facilitate individual and group conversations. Or how to talk with your family at shared meals or create safe discussions at the pub. Yet, any specific audience feels too narrow.

What we're here to do

In unpacking the Anatomy of Conversation, you will understand the elements of a quality conversation. There will be lots of practical things for you to do and plenty of considerations and reflections to deepen your practice. We will explore the words we say and the nuance of how we say them.

The disclaimer here is that facilitating conversations is intuitive, and you will learn faster the more you practice. Tune into your awareness of the different dynamics in a conversation. If this was a course on how to play music, I would provide you with the notes, but you must figure out how to play them and then do so with feeling. It is a skill and intuition that grows through practice.

My intent is for this book to provide a high-level introduction to the Anatomy of Conversation. It is designed to share the theory, flexibly and fittingly to any situation. More books may follow that specifically explore conversations with loved ones, with teammates, with family, with friends, with strangers and with ourselves. Most of the examples shared here are in a work setting, but they can easily be expanded and applied elsewhere.

Use this book like a field guide. Mark it up and reference often for any conversation opportunity. The tools in this book can work in individual, group, online and face-to-face conversations.

At this point, you might feel anxious at the thought of talking to people. Or perhaps you feel comfortable engaging with others. You might feel comfortable talking to your friends and no one else. No matter where you are on that spectrum of comfort, you can grow.

Conversation is a craft we continue to hone.

For you

Ultimately, this book is for you to improve your life by bringing courage into complex conversations.

Conversations can change your world. They help you to connect with others and find even more love. They create space to name what you want from others and express how you want to behave together or how you want to feel.

For any challenge, conversations and naming what is difficult starts us on the path. When we work together, we achieve more than the sum of our parts. Our connection holds us safely in exploration as we journey through inevitable change.

We are like pebbles. We smooth our edges when we rub against one another in the waves of change.

It all starts right now, with you. You have the power to ignite change through conversation, to move beyond fear and create stronger connections for all of us.

Key Terms

As we head into this space, I want to define several terms. Please note that I've tried to truncate the meanings; there are dozens of conversations and thoughts behind each word. My goal is to open your awareness to other ways of perceiving these buzzwords, so you might find your own alignment with them.

Diversity

Diversity is the recognition that we are all different.

When we have different perspectives participating, we create richer cultures. When we work together with our diverse experiences, we are more than our differences. We see new possibilities and gaps. Collaboration creates better outcomes.

Identity is important for self reflection and definition. We all have unique experiences that are informed by things both seen and unseen. We could name some of our differences such as skin tone, gender, sexual orientation, body and mind functionality. How we identify ourselves is infinitely varied.

I try to hold an intersectional perspective where there isn't a hierarchy of -isms, with one being worse than the other. I balance this with the awareness that whatever is most visible (skin colour, disability, gender) is often the primary frame for our identity. As someone with an intersection of dominant privileges, I navigate the world aware of these advantages. I try to hold these labels lightly in the spirit of connection and to avoid further division.

Inclusion

Inclusion is creating a safe place for everyone to express themselves fully and be accepted.

Safety means to be whole and unbroken. When we become more aware and listen beyond the words, we develop a sense of when our culture is cracking or broken. This can sound like sarcasm or complaining, or comments about feeling undervalued or wasting time. Addressing these head-on alleviates the pressure and slows the fracture; maybe it patches it up entirely.

My favourite quote from diversity consultant Verna Myers illustrates the difference between diversity and inclusion. 'Diversity is being invited to the party. Inclusion is being asked to dance.'[2]

Inclusion moves beyond identity labels into recognising the ecosystem we participate in, our shared culture and how it holds our differences. Some people use moral superiority or performative actions to prove how inclusive they are, but often those statements or activities isolate other people. We can't have inclusion with division.

Respect

Respect is mutual responsibility.

We are accountable to each other, especially when engaging in conversation. The phrase 'respectful conversations' is often used and infers that respect and conversations are inherently related. It is sometimes an explicit expectation, but more often, it is implicit. The challenge with implicit understanding is that it is easy to forget. It is assumed and thus falls into our unconscious mind and being. I want to make it explicit, to bring awareness to the meaning of respect, so we use it in our conversations.

This word 'respect' is variable. It differs from person to person, so our experiences, cultural practices and social norms don't always match. My attempt to define 'respect' is a stumbly version of 'how we treat others that allows and encourages them to be who they are, and mutually allows me to be who I am'. The Oxford Dictionary says respect is 'due regard for the feelings, wishes, or rights of others' and 'deep admiration for someone'.[3]

But even these definitions feel stale in the face of how expansive respect can be. Respect offers more questions than answers. How do you define it, and more importantly, how do you live respectfully? How do you ask and understand other people's expectations for respect?

Courage

Courage is having fear and taking a step anyway.

You are likely to feel fear going into difficult and sometimes messy conversations. It's ok. This is normal. Accept the fear and take a step anyway. Courageous action moves us beyond fear to meaningful connection. We have to cross the courage gap to get into deep conversation and reap the rewards.

We often hear the words 'courage' and 'bravery' used interchangeably, but they are different.

To me, bravery is an inherent character trait. It's something someone might have, and it can feel inaccessible if you don't.

Courage is something that we can all call upon.

For example, let's say you want to ask for a promotion at work. A brave person would swagger up with little preparation and lean on their strength of character to make the ask. In contrast, someone acting with courage would be hesitant and think through the situation to finally make a decision. That process of deciding lends extra strength to the action.

Courage is broken down into two root terms – 'cour' and 'age'. Cour is the Latin word for heart, the central organ that pumps blood throughout our bodies. In a meta sense, our hearts guide us and give feedback that we respond to. And our hearts can change. What or who we love one day might change the next. The second root word is 'age', meaning time.

If I'm being poetic, I'd say that your heart knows when it is time for courage. Listen to its call.

The Anatomy of Conversation

Overview

We're aiming for the golden conversation.

This is when every person and voice finds a groove and gently glides through the content you're discussing. You'll feel a warm, gooey, caramel feeling in your chest cavity. When the conversation has wrapped up, there will be a sense of completion and fullness. A deep satisfaction throughout your spirit. There's a sense of harmony – that all our different pieces fit together. Together, we are not alone in exploring our inner and outer worlds.

A golden conversation ends with these kinds of sentiments:

'Wow, thank you for sharing such a rich conversation.'
'I didn't realise how much that impacted me.'
'So much to consider!'
'Thank you, I feel seen and heard.'
'This went way better than I expected.'

Golden conversations are precious because they are infrequent. They are not the norm, but they are worth working towards having more often. One in five conversations is an incredible golden for me, and I've been practising for a while. When it happens, bask in it. Celebrate the sensation throughout your body, mind and spirit.

This golden conversation is what we are aiming for. That's what we'll explore in the Anatomy of Conversation.

Starting the fire

Consider the complexity and power of fire. It helps us survive and actively destroys. The power of fire is one of our basic needs, yet it also creates great harm when out of control. And that's ironic because you cannot control fire. You can nudge, entice, put out, feed and observe fire, but you cannot control it. You can prepare for the organic nature of fire by creating a ring to contain it and having a stack of wood or a bucket of water nearby. Conversations are similar.

This uncontrollable nature is one of the primary fears surrounding conversations. We cannot control the outcome. We can't know what the other person will do or how they will receive the conversation. All we can do is prepare ourselves, our mindsets and our questions, stories and information to navigate the conversation more confidently.

The facilitator of a conversation is the fire-keeper. We watch, listen and observe what the fire needs, then proactively adjust the fuel and oxygen to keep it burning steadily. If it flares up, we move the wood so it burns more evenly. If it starts to smoke, we add or change the fuel so it doesn't go out.

You don't force the conversation, hold responsibility for any responses, or make it satisfy a predetermined outcome. You guide a meaningful conversation for all. A golden conversation, gooey with connection, that radiates from within.

So, how do we start the fire? How do we start a conversation?

It starts with intention and decision. Are you committed to the process? There's no bowing out halfway through. Once you have decided, you can plan and prepare a structure before surrendering to the uncontrollable.

Opening a conversation is like starting a fire. How you set it up determines how it burns. With a fire, this might be how you stack your sticks. You might use newspaper or birch bark as the spark and kindling.

In a conversation, the opening set-up creates a safe and open tone, framing and setting clear expectations

---

You don't force the conversation, hold responsibility for any responses, or make it satisfy a pre-determined outcome.

You guide a meaningful conversation for all. A golden conversation, gooey with connection, that radiates from within.

---

together. We are separate entities when we start and we want to relieve that tension by finding common ground, spaces where we can be aligned.

The fire is going once the spark is lit and the kindling catches. It can burn as long as you feed it. In a conversation, once we know what we're here to discuss and how we will treat each other, once the open space of connection has been established, we enter the cadence of the conversation. While, in theory, a conversation can last as long as you like, I find it goes in waves and pockets. A meaningful conversation can last anywhere from 15 to 90 minutes. After that, creating a break and starting anew is often good if you have more to discuss.

A conversation consists of three activities – ask, listen and respond. It doesn't have to go exactly in that order or in an even balance; some conversations are more asking and listening than responding.

As a starting point, a great conversation pattern would be asking a question with curiosity, listening with care, and then responding with creativity. Rinse and repeat until you choose to close. It's the same with a fire; you keep adding fuel, observing the oxygen flow and adjusting the layout of the fire to keep it burning until you want to bring it to an end.

Let's define the three elements in the middle of a conversation.

Ask is the fuel of the conversation. Curiosity opens new territory for exploration, provides direction and signals that there is more to discuss and uncover. In a fire, it is adding fuel so it burns longer.

Listen involves observation and care. It is how we hear what is said and unsaid and interpret bodies, energy and tone. With a fire, it is observing the flow of oxygen throughout the nooks between logs. Watching how that creates a healthy, vibrant flame and consolidating the coals to better radiate heat.

Respond is how we creatively stitch together the conversation. We connect and reflect a positive summary of what was said. In a fire, we adjust the logs, using a stick to prod or lift and stack to create more airflow. It might be adjusting the footprint of the fire, depending on the needs of the gathering and the fire itself.

Ask, listen and respond. Weave these together to create a meaningful conversation. We can prepare questions, stories and responses, yet the true magic comes from listening to our intuition. Through practice, we grow our ability to understand when and how to engage.

And finally, our conversation comes to a close. Like a fire, an untended conversation can smoulder and burn into dangerous territory.

To close a conversation, we generously recap the key points and our common ground, ensuring everyone feels included and well-represented. Perhaps we leave with an ask or next step. At the fire, we rake the coals so they burn out or douse them with water.

There is a feedback loop in this style of conversation. Together, you are exploring, testing and talking explicitly about the content and how you are discussing it. Being receptive to this feedback helps navigate the conversation more easily because you know more of what is happening and are not acting from assumptions. Checking in repeatedly and asking for feedback creates a sense of buy-in or ownership from the participants because they are helping shape the experience.

You can ask for more or less of what you need at any point, continually updating expectations and explicitly naming what is required. You might suggest, 'Can you ask me a question?' or explain, 'I'm feeling bullied right now. Can we take a step back and remember we're here to discuss something that I have no control over.' The facilitator is in an inherently different role from the participants, but your feedback is also valuable. As the person shepherding the conversation, you, too, can explicitly name what you need to navigate the conversation comfortably.

Feedback is precious, as it helps us learn, adapt and improve. Receive feedback with openness and grace. If you respond defensively (something I continue to work on unlearning), it prevents others from sharing future feedback until you've rebuilt trust. In the Respond section, we will go deeper on providing and utilising feedback.

Guiding values

If the anatomy of a conversation gives its structure, how do we define the essence? When is it more than bones? A fire is merely a pile of combusting fuel, so why does it draw us in and compel us to gather and connect?

Values and beliefs guide our lives. Four core values or ways of being facilitate meaningful conversations — Generosity, Love, Openness and Wonder. You simply have to **GLOW**.

Over time, you'll develop intuition for managing the essence of a conversation. Practising these four values starts with awareness of the dynamics and your role in influencing them. Then, you take further responsibility and assert your personal variations of generosity, love, openness and wonder. Try different approaches to see what works for you. Develop your unique way of facilitating golden conversations.

At each conversation stage, we link practical actions to these core values. These actions are often verbal, with examples of dialogue and responses. Sometimes they are non-verbal, communicated with body, gestures and tone, or related to our intentions. The emphasis of this book is on interactive conversations in real-time, whether in-person, over the phone or online. Of course, some of the principles can apply to your emails, messages and social media posts.

For now, let's define and work through these values.

– Generosity –

Generosity means giving — of yourself, your material possessions or your time and energy. Specifically, it means to give more than is expected. To go above the minimum requirement and to give or do more.

What is most generous about this value is that when we give, we also receive. We feel a sense of fulfilment by helping others. Even simple things. For example, do you smile when you pass a stranger in your neighbourhood? It is free and provides so much value. The other person feels seen and acknowledged, and you both feel the warmth of connection.

In our conversations, a sense of generosity helps all feel comfortable and welcome. Hospitality is another way to think about this.

On Being is a podcast hosted by Krista Tippett which explores 'animating questions at the centre of human life: What does it mean to be human, and how do we want to live?' The episodes are a masterclass in exploratory conversations seeking common ground. On Being's *Better Conversations Guide* demonstrates how hospitality and conversations are connected.[4] It says, 'Hospitality is a bridge to all the great virtues, but it is immediately accessible. You don't have to love or forgive or feel compassion to extend hospitality.'

Hospitality can be extending care for everyone's physical needs, such as drinks and comfortable seating, ensuring optimum comfort. To be a great host, greet people generously and assure them they will be considered and cared for.

– Generosity **Love** Openness Wonder –

Love is the ultimate renewable resource. It provides infinite energy, powering us forward. And yet, our society has largely relegated love to the confines of romantic love. We treat it as finite and scarce, only to be given to those we trust. Yet when we realise love is infinite, we begin to access an ever-growing pool of power within ourselves.

In her book *all about love*, bell hooks makes a passionate case for embedding love in our culture, saying, 'Only love can heal the wounds of the past'.[5] hooks' offer of a 'hopeful, joyous vision of love's transformative power' moved me deeply and expanded my understanding of what it means to participate in a loving culture.

We all need love. To feel love, and to be loved. We can access this through self-love, the love of others, love for our experiences and the world around us. Love is everywhere.

Love helps us to see and be seen. This unconditional acceptance of our whole selves frees us from judgement and fear that often stand in the way of change.

To truly live, we must love.

Love is essential for connection. It is the matter connection is made of. That's not to say you must love all those you are connected to, but the possibility of love and love for yourself brings you into connection with others.

Courage is at the heart of love. It is courageous to open your heart and to be vulnerable.

Bringing love into your conversations is a courageous act. Nelson Mandela said, 'I never lose, I either win or learn'. Removing the binary of win/lose is a helpful reminder that action teaches us. Especially courageous action.

So go forth courageously; go forward with love!

Action teaches us.
Especially courageous action.

– Openness –

Openness creates a safe space that enables vulnerability. An unbroken place where each person feels they belong to the whole and that the whole of them is accepted.

Take note of when the sense of safety begins to waver or crack and address those fissures straight away. Simply naming your observation can be the starting point. *'I noticed your body language changed when I said that. What happened for you? What are you feeling?'* It gives you more information so you can learn about or address what has changed.

Repairing a crack is much easier than rejoining two completely broken pieces. It can feel intense to ask about the awkward or sticky stuff that people are feeling, but the sooner it is voiced the better. Once you understand what they need, you can work to patch it up. Know that talking about any fractures will create a better outcome in the long term. Harness your courage to name what's broken so that it may be repaired.

Become comfortable with awkward silences. They happen. All the time.

Remember, though, you cannot help people if they do not want to be helped. Watch for when someone voices their objections, but instead of changing or moving on, they hold on to it with a vice grip. They are on their own journey of acceptance, worthiness and self-love. Give them a chance to express and change, but if they are truly stuck, continue the conversation and name it as you go.

'We're about to discuss timeliness. At the beginning, you mentioned how stressed you were because you don't have a car and taking the bus is too unpredictable. I understand that, and let's still explore other avenues to be more accountable to the timelines we set.'

While it is your responsibility as the facilitator to create and maintain an open and safe space, many things are outside your control.

– Generosity Love Openness Wonder –

Wonder is both a noun and a verb.

The noun describes a marvellous thing, magnificent, an object of admiration. The verb directly relates to curiosity or doubt. I like how these interplay – perhaps we can approach each person as a magical, mystical being that we don't understand. We then follow our curiosity to find out more, invoking an approach to conversation outside our logical brain and tapping more into our hearts and spirits.

Remember how curious and full of wonder you were as a child? It seems that much of my adult life has been unlearning the constraints I have applied since my teenage years. I seek to return to that spirit of childlike wonder. The real trick is maintaining adult responsibilities while maintaining a joyful and curious outlook.

So, what is curiosity? The Oxford Dictionary defines it as 'a strong desire to know something' [6] but this explanation feels wooden compared to the magic I feel when I am curious. When I am curious, I feel electric, alive with tingling anticipation, seeking to satisfy a hunger. Voracious, sniffing it out, blind to distractions. Serendipitously stumbling across a surprise satisfies the child within.

Wonder is entwined with learning. If curiosity drives us forward, wonder and learning are the process, and the prize is wisdom.

When I am curious about other people, I'm looking through a kaleidoscope and marvelling at how each twist changes the picture. Each person has many shapes and colours inside. I want to see beyond the

If curiosity drives us forward,
learning is the process,
and the prize is wisdom.

facade they present externally. Whenever I get a peek at someone's internal world, I am in awe.

Our curiosity is unique. What you find interesting is different from what I find interesting. Thus, we could start the same conversation on the same topic and end up in completely different places.

For example, in a conversation about responding to emails, one person might focus on communication and social anxiety pressures, while another might want to discuss the amazing advantages of electronic communication compared with paper-based offices. They may even find solidarity in the crush of too many emails. And, of course, there will be a multitude of responses between.

Wonder is the recognition of the infinite possibilities of you, me and us together. There are infinite combinations of interactions between people.

Wonder in conversations is seeking to understand, turning over every rock and exploring every idea from every angle to understand something thoroughly.

Chasing wonder is like following a thread of light – what sparks you? What do you want to explore next?

Go there.

Open
Respond
Ask
Listen
Close

Generosity
love
Openness
Wonder

Open

When deciding to set a fire, you must first prepare the area. Clear the space and create a boundary to ensure the fire doesn't get out of hand. Gather the materials: a stack of dry wood and a bucket of water.

To start the fire, we need an initial structure. Start with an anchor log at the back. Along one side, add some tinder or flammable material near the base. Above this, gently place twigs and slightly larger sticks, with the thinnest twigs closest to the tinder and moving up in size and thickness. Flames burn upwards, so this way, larger pieces of wood catch fire and burn on their own.

Now we light the fire!

The conversation begins when you decide to have a meaningful or challenging conversation. It doesn't start when you open your mouth to speak.

This action is what we need to reset. We can actively decide to have meaningful conversations and then prepare for them with conviction and intent.

That decision allows us to dive into the sometimes scary and unknown space between us. Deciding to have a conversation is the decision to air our beliefs, preferences and experiences. There are certainly risks, but we stand to gain greater ease and connection.

The conversation begins when you decide to have a meaningful or challenging conversation.

It doesn't start when you open your mouth to speak.

Many things can go wrong if we don't intentionally open conversations. The tone you start with determines how the rest of the conversation flows. How you open creates a knock-on effect. There is momentum to conversations where everything builds on itself.

It goes wrong when you (as the facilitator) come into the conversation with a negative attitude. Perhaps you think you're right and you want to prove others wrong. Or maybe you think they are guilty or stupid. You bring in a predetermined idea and set up the conversation to align with your bias. Naturally, this causes others to withdraw because they don't like being persuaded or put on trial. Why should they bother? Why waste time and effort if you are unwilling to change your mind? We have to bring openness and embrace the unknowns and possibilities. That enables true and honest conversation to emerge.

Starting can also go wrong when logistics get in the way. It could be a noisy room or a distracting environment. It's difficult to consider their responses when your attention keeps getting hijacked by the surface-level environment. This situation will naturally limit the depth and meaning of the conversation.

If you do start a conversation the wrong way and it feels all weird, you can recover and reset. It just takes a bit of time and effort. You can navigate this explicitly

---

Deciding to have a conversation is the decision to air our beliefs, preferences and experiences.

---

by saying, *'I feel like I didn't start off well. Can we go back to the beginning and try again?'* Or by taking a physical break; *'I feel like this started the wrong way. I'd like to take a break and meet again later. Is that all right with you?'*

When you honestly assess the situation and name the tension or emotion they are also feeling, you honour the experience, make them feel validated in that raw emotion, and recruit them to help it go better the next time. You could even ask for feedback at this point, *'Hey I think we started this off all wrong, and I'd like to try again. Do you have any feedback for me to consider before we pick it back up and try again?'* Remember to respond with grace and try not to be defensive. We can choose to take it personally and make it about us, or we can take a breath and orient towards a mindset of service. What does this person need? How can I be of service to their experience?

Opening a conversation is about trust and building connection as the foundation for everything that follows. We **GLOW** in the opening of a conversation when we embody generosity by being caring and considerate of their needs, open our hearts and respond with love instead of judgement, create a sense of safety and wonder at all the possibilities for the conversation we are about to co-create. Combining these elements creates a solid environment for connection and exploration to thrive.

– Generosity Love Openness Wonder –

A conversation starts from our first awareness of each other.

The initial greeting and body language should ooze generosity, warmth and hospitality. A genuine welcome releases fear and uncertainty and allows people to relax. Even if the mind is cynical in its response, genuine hospitality always overrules and the body eases in.

To embody generosity when opening a conversation, focus on your initial greeting with positivity, openness and kindness. Set the tone of connection early.

There's a formulaic cultural exchange of greetings which goes, *'Hi, how are you?' 'Hi, I'm good, thanks, how are you?' 'I'm fine, thanks.'* It passes back and forth as a ritual without any consideration for how we truly are. There is no substance. Instead, use this perfect moment to pause and genuinely check in with the other person. *'You didn't sound fine, what's up?'* or *'How are you really?'* or you might need to lead it, saying, *'I said I'm good, but really I'm (bubbly/tired/silly/anxious/insert true emotion here) because of...'.*

Sometimes, I pause to think aloud. *'Hmm, how am I really? Let me take a second and check in... actually,*

I'm feeling ....' From those first words we exchange, let us be honest with ourselves and those we meet with. This pause evokes presence; it brings you into the now. Being present enables better participation.

The next move might sound obvious, yet we forget its power. Smile. A smile communicates intent without a single word. You don't need to fake a big toothy smile from the movies; it's more important to work on finding your true smile.

Try this in front of a mirror: close your eyes and think about a time when you've been full of joy. Maybe when your friend was acting silly a few weeks ago or the way a loved one says your name. Without changing a thing, open your eyes and observe how beautiful your smile is. It might be full of dimples and teeth; it might be a subtle twist at the corner; it might even reach your eye creases. This smile is lovely and it is yours.

Another option is to think about the person you're conversing with. Remember how much you love them and want the best for them — as we should desire for any fellow human being. Feel their humanity, the fragility and fallibility of our experience, and open your heart towards them with compassion and acceptance. Open your eyes and share that smile with them when you meet for your conversation.

Sometimes, if the situation is tense, it feels hard to bring a smile. Fake it 'til you make it, without going over the top. Bring humour or levity into the conversation so everyone can take a brief respite and crack a grin. Lighten the mood — if only for an instant.

Another key concept here is hospitality. Care for your guest's comfort. Ask if they need a glass of water or a more comfortable chair. Listen to how their day has been so far. Observe and receive their energy, but don't smother them or be overly attentive. When you notice them repeatedly refusing, *'No, I'm all right, thank you, I don't need anything more'*, dial it back so it doesn't become a nag.

Sometimes, we use service to delay starting the conversation. There is a timing balance – you want them to be comfortable, have time to become present and be ready to participate, but you also don't want them to have to sit in awkwardness or anticipation for too long.

The time before the conversation starts can almost be worse because we're waiting in suspense, especially if we don't know what the conversation is about. Be kind, make them feel comfortable and then get into it.

Consider the environment for the conversation. If you have a choice, go where you both are comfortable and can hear each other. It should be a place where you can engage without distraction or barriers (mental, physical or emotional). It doesn't have to be a formal setting. My favourite space for challenging conversations is doing a walk-and-talk where we walk side-by-side (or even over the phone). This facilitates a non-oppositional space instead of me-against-you talking over a table, and the activity of walking allows space to think. You don't need to respond immediately; you can do 'walking', which buys time for reflection without creating an awkward silence.

A note here: Be considerate of the actual tone of the conversation, not how you desire it.

A while ago, I visited a corporate office where they had a cool couch chill space. I commented on how great that would be for facilitating connection and getting out of formality. The person I was chatting with agreed it was great for those occasions, but she'd also heard of people getting performance feedback and even fired out there.

The space would have been totally confusing – are we here to chill or be serious? If I had been a participant in a feedback conversation there, the tone of a relaxed, chill environment would have felt almost disrespectful to the gravity of the topic. I would have been confused and caught off guard. I imagine the manager was trying to make them feel more comfortable, but complex conversations can be uncomfortable. We need to honour the real experience, not try to sugar coat or make it less difficult through a friendly environment, bribes of food and drink or vague words that tell half-truths.

- love -

Opening a conversation with love invites you to judge less. Whatever they're wearing, how they behave, smell or speak, however different you think you are, try to suspend your judgement. See them for the human being, the fallible, magical, perfect human they are, just like you.

When interacting with the world around us, judgement can be useful. We're hardwired to judge situations for self-protection, but judgement runs rampant in our relatively comfortable modern world. We judge others in the blink of an eye and then hold these initial impressions as the truth. Even when many of these judgements are imagined, shaped by our experiences, our stories of self and social conditioning.

Our social norms are deeply and often unconsciously embedded. As you become aware of your beliefs, begin to examine them. Where do they root from? Whose voice do you hear sharing this idea? Objectively and within my own heart, do I believe this or that? Have compassion for yourself — rewiring this software doesn't happen overnight.

Reflecting on your biases and judgements happens in and around the conversation. You might prepare by

When engaging with someone on a topic, be mindful of where they are on the spectrum of belief.

Instead of trying to immediately convert them to your position, meet them where they are at.

questioning your initial judgement of the person and situation. Break them down and identify the roots.

For example, you might judge someone as lazy, as you always see them talking to other staff. When you stop and think, do you judge them because you were once called lazy for standing around chatting? Perhaps it's because you wish you had more time and space to connect with your colleagues. Or maybe you are frustrated that you're always waiting for their work to be done so that you can do your part. These diverse reasons could all stem from the unexamined belief that they are lazy.

Knowing this helps you better understand your motives for shaping the conversation. A useful or productive conversation can be achieved if you're aware that you're frustrated. You can voice that feeling and work to find solutions rather than having a conversation that won't satisfy your needs and to which they will respond defensively.

When engaging with someone on a topic, be mindful of where they are on the spectrum of belief. Instead of trying to immediately convert them to your position, meet them where they are at. Gently and from a place of understanding, walk with them and encourage them to consider different perspectives. This might even shift their thinking.

For example, you might talk with someone about the organisation's diversity and inclusion policy. Perhaps they think it's all a bunch of woke nonsense and are actively triggered by the words. In the conversation, verbalise the policy and your expectations of their behaviour with strength and commitment. Enter this conversation gently rather than with force. Some would start this conversation by saying, *'The world has moved on and your outdated ways of thinking and doing are wrong'.* You might not use such frank words, but if that is your intent, then no matter what words you use, that's how they will hear it.

Instead, come at it from a more basic level. Meet them where they're at and build from there. That might sound like, *'Remember in school when we're taught to be kind and not hit or kick people? This is similar in that we want to ensure we aren't hurting people and that everyone feels safe here. I understand that hurting might not be your intent, but that is what is happening when you say or do these things. What is your intent when you say or do these things?'*

This example meets them in their space using words they can relate to. It also puts the onus back on them to help you understand their position and motivation. Using this information, you can craft a response to their specific barriers, questions or needs. The balance here is not to use condescending language.

It's a courageous act of love not to let someone be lonely in their opinion, and instead to put your feelings aside and stand in solidarity towards greater awareness and exploration.

Over time, your conversation craft and intuition will develop to meet others where they are and find common ground. It's a courageous act of love not to let someone be lonely in their opinion, and instead to put your feelings aside and stand in solidarity towards greater awareness and exploration.

Judgement is tricky and embedded. Once you know when you are responding with judgement, you can choose love instead. It takes time to listen to your heart, but it does become easier. Ultimately, when we choose love, our souls are light.

Creating a space of openness and safety starts with you. When you share vulnerably, you open up a space for others to join. You have to lead the way. Model the depth and openness of how you want them to participate.

It can be simple, like sharing how you really are. *'How am I going? Well, I'm feeling a little overwhelmed today with back-to-back meetings.'* Or *'I'm feeling really inspired because I love having conversations with people about how they want to grow and develop.'*

It is simple to demonstrate what a genuine answer sounds like to a formulaic question. Some people may be taken aback by your honesty, as many go through the motions without considering their true status, let alone how others are.

Be aware of what might be too much information. This is contextual. Talking with your best friend is very different from how you'd express yourself with your boss or at a formal event. Consider your audience and find the balance to achieve honesty and connection.

Opening the conversation with a complex story shares your experiences, but it must be contextually relevant. For example, if your conversation is to provide feedback on engaging with stakeholders, talk about when you first learned how to communicate, email, phone and run meetings or workshops with those groups. Perhaps recount when you made a mistake, created an awkward moment or had some negative consequences.

Sharing stories like this is valuable. It demonstrates that you understand their experience and opens a space to say mistakes are ok — we learn from our mistakes. And most importantly, it confirms that it's ok to talk about learning. Sharing stories and experiences builds understanding and empathy.

There is a balance with vulnerable storytelling. Just because you are comfortable talking about heavy stuff doesn't necessarily mean others are, so gauge your level of vulnerability. Aim for courageous but not too challenging. In the previous example of starting a conversation to provide feedback, don't tell of a time when you miscommunicated with a stakeholder and got fired. If I heard that story, I'd be terrified that I might suffer the same consequence, and I would clam up.

Opening a safe and inclusive conversation space is situational because each person has their own baggage and orientation to building trust and connection. For some, that space opens easily, while

Your posture should demonstrate openness and an eagerness to receive.

with others, you might only ever get a shallow view. There are no right or wrong answers. We must meet everyone where they're at and try to be a bit more open — if only a notch.

What if they don't want to join the conversation with open intent? Some people are super-sensitive and always feel slighted. You can never do or say enough for them to feel included. This can be a symptom of ego, where they and their labels are the most precious and can take up space at the expense of inclusion. Some are so convinced they are right that they have closed their eyes and ears. They shout their opinions and call it truth. I think we all need to loosen our grasp on our ego and extend each other some grace.

One last consideration when opening a conversation is non-verbal communication. While this is mostly about body language, also consider distractions. If you're creating an intentionally safe space for honest conversation, checking notifications on your devices breaks the link between you. It's one of the reasons I wear an old fashioned analogue watch because it helps me keep time without involving a screen and other inputs outside this conversation or workshop. My watch is a key part of my facilitator gear.

Your posture should demonstrate openness and an eagerness to receive. My go-to (originally unintentional but now deliberate) is to lean forward, my hands open or fingers loosely threaded. That loose shape models an intent of ease and rest for them. Think about what shapes you would feel most comfortable and uncomfortable sitting across from. I feel defensive when the other person crosses their arms or we sit across the table like adversaries. Tune into your body and what feels open to you. Let your body be your teacher. Like most things, we each have preferences that feel right for us.

Conversations are one-time moments that we share with others. No two conversations are ever the same, and each person's unique experiences and energy contribute to that magic. Involving everyone in creating the expectations and desired outcomes assures them that you are aligned and heading into the conversation to tackle the problem or question together.

When building a conversation, start with expectations. Set explicit guidelines for how you will interact, your shared purpose for this conversation and where you hope to arrive. This provides everyone with the expected norms and allows them to relax into the flow, knowing where they are headed. Co-create the rules of engagement.

Building expectations together creates buy-in. For each expectation set, ask for confirmation or feedback. This creates an explicit agreement and allows them to say what they might need more (or less) of to engage.

Getting each person to agree on how to treat each other is a psychological process that creates a social contract. Set simple expectations like *'Let's agree not to interrupt each other. If we think someone has been talking for too long, we can raise a hand and, if others agree, the person talking will wrap up. How does that sound?'* Or make it more nuanced. *'We know there are disagreements in how we proceed, let's agree not to make any personal attacks. Can we all agree on that?'*

You might start wide open and let them lead the design. *'I wonder how we want to conduct this conversation. Any suggestions for ground rules?'*

Setting expectations can also happen throughout the conversation.

If you start down a path that requires explicit framing or expectations, simply propose a new expectation and get further confirmation.

For example, *'we're heading down a path describing our families. Let's agree that every family is different and no one way is the right way. We all think our way is the right way. Let's go into this from a perspective of sharing our different ways of doing this, rather than attacking how others do it. How's that sound?'*

One of my favourite expectations comes from speaker and author Lisa O'Neill. It is especially useful for online conversations where people feel a greater sense of distance.

Before going into breakout rooms, Lisa reminds people to co-facilitate the conversation, 'Don't be a hog or a log', meaning don't hog the space and talk the whole time, and don't sit back and be a passive observer. It is a brilliant little quip to switch people into becoming more active participants.

When imagining how the conversation will flow, consider the desired objective. By discussing where you hope to end up, you build the conversation with the end in mind. That could sound like, *'I hope we find a satisfying resolution we're both content with',* or *'Let's discuss and decide on a transition plan that accommodates all our needs'*.

The desired objective is general enough to allow concrete responses to emerge, but specific in the tone of collaboration. That is where you can set us up to work together towards the objective, problem or question.

Ask

Fire needs fuel to burn. Adding logs feeds the fire. The placement of the logs should complement the existing fire structure, keeping it balanced and burning evenly. Adding wet wood will stall the burn, create smoke and be unpleasant. Typically, add one log at a time, then wait for it to catch and burn down a bit before adding another.

In a conversation, questions are the fuel. They keep the conversation going and adjust the direction of the discussion by elevating or focusing on a specific area. In murky, complex or heated conversations, asking questions helps us better understand the various perspectives and emotions. We can find new links, options and pathways using the information we gather.

When trying to find connection and common ground, questions are the answer. Questions are fuelled by curiosity. Our intent is to explore every person's unique experiences, observations, feelings and thoughts.

Two people can go through the same events, share the same facts and make it mean two completely different things. Searching for these meanings is raw and rewarding. We consciously realise the stories we tell ourselves and thus are free to embrace or change the story.

When trying to find connection and common ground, questions are the answer.

We seek to understand rather than cast judgement on the responses. When we ask questions with genuine love and curiosity, people open up and share answers that might even surprise them. Bringing our subconscious or internal world into the external world through communication is a transformative experience. Being witness to it is an honour and a gift.

Asking questions encourages others to add to the shared pool of learning. This concept is from the book *Crucial Conversations* by Patterson, Grenny, McMillan and Switzler.[7] It encourages all participants to contribute information so everyone has a shared and explicit understanding of what is going on, what it means and how it makes them feel. This transparency helps create shared understanding, explain common themes, and help facilitate the exploration of gaps or things that don't make sense. None of this is possible without a common pool of knowledge that all can access.

You might be stuck on how to be curious. You understand the meaning of curiosity, but how do you practice it? There are several approaches. We'll outline how questions and curiosity weave throughout **GLOW**. In the wonder of exploration, we'll consider how we ask questions with generosity and love and which styles of questioning are more open.

Before we get into how to ask well, we must name the risks of when asking goes wrong.

Asking can turn into an interrogation, where we feel pelted by questions. This makes others feel like they are being attacked, as there is no space for reflection or considered responses. They start firing back equally quick and pointed answers or even shut down entirely. There is pacing and spacing to questions, and much like a fire, if you add too many too quickly, the conversation will burn bigger and hotter and maybe even get out of control. It's better to consider which log to place where, and when to ask a question or follow-up.

Ask can also go wrong when we ask pointed questions or don't want hear the answer. It's the fastest way to dead-end a conversation. A pointed question evokes a defensive response. If you don't want to hear the answer, you stop listening, thus putting out the fire.

We'll cover specific examples in the following sections.

Asking generous questions offers a positive approach to enquiry. It allows others to interpret and respond in various ways, empowering them to choose the direction. Generous questions are open in content and tone, allowing the person to respond in ways that are favourable to them.

Creating good questions is a skill that gets better with practice. Writing questions in advance is one of the strongest ways to prepare for a difficult conversation. When you're in the chaos of conversation and don't know where to go next, having a few quality questions is helpful. They also keep your facilitation aligned with your intention rather than being influenced by emotion or as a reaction to something said. Our intent is to explore together, not cause pain. We are united in this exploration and discovery; it's not you versus me.

Questions are greatly undervalued and underappreciated. Some cultures are neither comfortable nor skilled at asking questions. We rely instead on shared experience to provide conversation fodder. That is fine, but it's not deep connection.

When asking questions, be aware of your intent. If your aim is to prove something, or to make them feel bad, then reconsider. We've all been on the receiving end of a question designed to be sharp, poke or make us react. Interrogation doesn't feel good and creates a defensive environment, which is the opposite of an open and safe space.

Here's an extreme example:

'Why do you think that butchering our planet is ok?' (Exaggerated language puts the other person in a bad light.)

Instead, try this:

'Why do you think we should compromise on environmental protection?' (Strong. Framed as a compromise and acknowledges complexity and trade-offs while still inviting response.)

And a more subtle example:

'Why didn't you get that document on time to me like I asked?' (Makes me feel bad for letting you down, slightly aggressive tone.)

Try this instead:

'Why was the document late?' (Open to whatever answer.)

As you note, open questions are simpler, with fewer words and more direct.

Less generous questions are leading, sharp and pokey, pushing or forcing the conversation or person into a set response. It shuts down the conversation quickly. After all, why bother having a chat if the answer seems predetermined?

Love in our questions allows for compassion. We ask questions openly, seeking and seeing our shared humanity. It means you ask questions from your heart while being aware of your and others' emotions rather than strictly logic-driven enquiry. Empathy reinforces safety and encourages everyone to be more honest in their responses. Love encourages us to speak to our shared connections and commonalities as humans.

When you ask questions, your tone is important, as often we aren't aware of how we're saying something. You know when you ask a question and all the right words are there, but the person responds unexpectedly or defensively? That is because of tone. Our voices are musical instruments and convey so much.

In simple terms, tone consists of the pitch (how high or low the notes are) and the force (how high or low the volume is). As you develop an awareness of tone, you can become nuanced and specific in adjusting your voice to convey a point.

To start, focus on the force of your tone. If you want to emphasise something, say it a bit louder. To draw them in, speak more gently.

Empathy reinforces safety and encourages everyone to be more honest in their responses.

Consider how your pitch changes throughout the questions or statements. Does your voice go up or down? Many Australians use statement questions with an upward inflection as if that suddenly makes it a question. *'Let's get a coffee before this meeting (upward inflection)'* is not the same as *'Would you like to get a coffee before the meeting?'*, which has a direct question word.

Tone has spectrums of nuance, but this is enough to get started and, as with many things, you will observe and adjust simply by being aware.

The tone we want to embody in our conversations is gentle enquiry. We go into it humbly without judgement and seek to understand. Each human being is unique. Every person has something valuable to share. You don't want to go in with your walls up or embrace a power dynamic that makes you better than them. That creates a tone of moral superiority, a tone that divides us. Instead, seek to discover what is valuable about them, so you see them as they are and maybe even find a sense of love.

We can be aligned with love in our body language as well. For example, be sensitive to the power dynamics of where everyone is sitting. A shared power setting is often the best because it encourages everyone to participate as equals. In some conversations, you might want to physically demonstrate your power by sitting at the head of the table or in a slightly elevated position. In my experience, embracing yourself as the facilitator in any setting is enough to establish your authority.

Open-ended questions are the main questions to use in conversations. Closed questions that are answered by a simple 'Yes' or 'No' often lead through a stilted conversation that feels like filling out a form. Instead, open-ended questions usually start with 'Who', 'What', 'Where', 'When', 'Why' or 'How'. When designing your question, consider the answer you want because each of these question words will evoke a different response. Here's an example.

'Who made you feel that way?'

> *'Taylor.'*

'What made you feel that way?'

> *'It was when Jo said...'*

'Where did you feel that way?'

> *'Here at work, in that meeting.'*

'When did you feel that way?'

> *'It happened in the meeting when they said that and I felt it right away...'*

'Why did you feel that way?'

'Because they were saying I did the thing and I didn't...'

'How did that make you feel?'

'I felt attacked and angry.'

Generating questions and considering the possible responses helps you think through and plan the different directions in which the conversation can flow. That is not so you can be rigid or go in with expectations; it's more to help you prepare for situations that might evolve from what the other person says. When imagining responses, don't just focus on the negative or worst-case scenarios; consider the full spectrum of responses – positive, negative, confused, apathetic, etc.

Openness is seeking to understand. It often leads me to try and patch up holes in what someone is saying, particularly if I don't understand their point or how it relates to our topic. A simple go-to phrase asking them to explain further is saying, *'Tell me more?'* which helps me gather more data and information to understand better.

Being in wonder means being open to surprise.

Asking open questions allows the other person to respond with infinite possibilities. We can't know what they will say. If we hold no expectations, we go in as a blank slate. No matter what the response, it will feel unique and wonderful.

One of my key tactics is to embrace the humble learner mindset and pretend I know nothing. When I am in a conversation, it sometimes helps to remind myself that I don't know the answer and to open myself up to the possibility of surprise.

Another skill is to tune into what you are personally interested in. For example, I am learning about feelings, part of a longer process of moving from my head into my heart. So, when asking people about their lives, I often enquire, *'How did that make you feel?'* or *'How would you describe how you felt then?'* Feelings naturally lead to the heart space, so I end up in some quite deep conversations.

I go through phases and have different fun questions for social gatherings. I'm a positive idealist and my questions for social environments reflect this.

At a bachelorette night, I asked, *'If you could wave a magic wand and change one thing in our society, what would it be?'* We shared a rich chat over suggestive cocktails.

To start, I say, *'I'm doing an informal focus group and asking people…'* which immediately sets the tone for play. Play spaces have no expectations and no judgement. They encourage randomness and silliness and feel joyful.

Over the years, I've asked, *'Where is home for you and how do you define home?' 'How do we reconcile our need for technology and resources and ensuring sustainability for our planet?'* (that one gets a bit heated). My personal favourite for many years, pre-pandemic, was *'We're overpopulated as a planet, how would you resolve that problem?'* Yes, I'm super fun at parties.

This principle can be applied to anyone – perhaps you enjoy art, video games or fishing. Those activities are about expression, exploration, contemplation, achievement, reflection, peace and quiet — all qualities you can chase curiously through almost any context or content of conversation.

At this point, you might pause and realise that you don't know what you like or how to describe it.

Play spaces have no expectations and no judgement. They encourage randomness and silliness and feel joyful.

In an interview with Bill Maher, relationships expert Esther Perel said 'You learn to love yourself in the context of your relationships with others. The idea that you go to work on yourself here and prepare this package is completely off. It is interactive; you need an amount of self-awareness, but it is through interactions with others that you become aware. Other people let you see who you are, it's by being with others that you get to know who you are.'[8]

So, open yourself to the possibility that your thread of curiosity will be uncovered through more courageous conversations.

listen

A fire is not something you can set and forget. It needs constant supervision and care by the firekeeper. As the flames crackle and pop, pay attention to ensure the fire continues burning merrily. Look for dead zones where the flame or heat has reduced. Is it because there is too much airflow and oxygen? Or not enough? Is there insufficient fuel, or are the logs too concentrated in one area?

The fire is under constant observation and optimisation. Keep holding it in your awareness. We're aiming for a smoke-free, crackling fire that radiates heat. Because the primary function is destruction, it will continue to change and evolve shape. Nothing is permanent or guaranteed in a fire; we must watch for any changes and adjust accordingly.

It's the same with a conversation. As the firekeeper and facilitator of the discussion, you hold the space and can navigate the conversation in any direction. Your goal is to maintain the quality of open dialogue, absorbing any awkwardness or discomfort and navigating back towards common ground.

Listening is perhaps the most obvious part of a conversation, yet it is an underdeveloped practice in our modern culture.

I love the saying attributed to the Greek philosopher Epictetus, 'We have two ears and one mouth, so we can listen twice as much as we speak.' In my conversations, I aim to hit an 80:20 ratio. That's listening 80% of the time and talking or asking the other 20%. The more I listen, the more I learn, and the better I can shape the conversation towards common ground.

The skill of listening is hard, and declining attention spans are making it more difficult in our digitally connected society. Listening is like a muscle, but our capacity can grow with more reps and practice.

Through deep listening, we discover individual perspectives and unique value. Everyone has something valuable within them, but often, it has been turned down by themselves or others. Everyone has value, and everyone has potential. Just as you believe this for yourself, so should you believe this is true for everyone. That belief will spark curiosity about any human and push you deeper into listening.

Listening is not just processing sounds with your ears; it is deep observation of what is said and unsaid, and the tonal shifts in the body as information and stories are revealed.

When you listen with your whole self, you absorb the other person more fully. You can better empathise and understand their perspective to meet and explore together. This is an active process, not passive, as

When you listen with your whole self, you absorb the other person more fully.

many imagine. A lot is going on in the background. It might not feel like much, but practising deep listening and holding the space for someone is tiring. Energy filling and physically tiring, as odd as that combination might seem.

When we **GLOW** while listening, we extend them some grace. Give them the generosity of space to work out what they mean, assume positive intent with open body language and follow your curiosity.

Listening generously means giving others space to figure things out. Deep conversations can reveal layers of self-reflection that many have not visited or explored before. It might be the first time they have thought about or felt this. It might be the first time they've externalised by saying it aloud, and often it's the first time they've said it to another person.

Everyone is rewarded when you are patient and give them space to consider and verbalise something they feel. They go through the joy of self-discovery and self-knowing, and you get the pleasure of receiving an honest human response. What an honour to see someone as they are, the raw parts of our human existence. Together, you discover new territories within, and it is deeply rewarding.

This exploration also reveals new information — new data points beyond what we could have imagined or judged to be true. At these deeper layers, surprise is common. Not surprise at a dramatic reveal; it's often at the mundane or simple human truths.

Some I've heard over the years are:

'Wow, I didn't realise how much working with numbers on Excel gave me such purpose and joy. I

guess I thought it was weird to like accounting, but I actually love it!'

'Hmm, I didn't realise that interrupting people was linked to my deep desire to be liked. I'm always seeking approval from other people and interrupting is how I insert that ...'

'Huh, my love of history relates back to reading with my dad as a kid. That's where it started!'

In our modern world, we're always rushing or under time pressure. Conversations are a brilliant container for exploring ourselves with others. Creating that space for self-reflection is a gift. To give someone your time and share energy mirroring and helping each other to know ourselves, our beliefs and our behaviours better. This process cannot be rushed; it requires patience, care and generosity.

By giving our time and energy, we help each other to better know ourselves, our beliefs and our behaviours.

Listening with love invites us to assume positive intent. When we listen to others, we often jump to judgements, which create an emotional reaction. Instead, and especially if you disagree, assume positive intent while listening. Don't simply look for opportunities to pounce and attack.

Assuming positive intent is especially important when dealing with complex and variable topics, such as culture. Defining culture and how we participate in a shared culture is different for every person, every team, every group, every organisation and every community. Listening and understanding each other is how we identify our common ground – where connection and love flourish.

Have you ever been in a situation where the words come out all wrong? Or where someone takes offence to a single word and doesn't acknowledge the surrounding context? When having difficult conversations, it can be helpful to explicitly create a rule to assume positive intent so people can freely share. That doesn't mean offensive or bigoted language is allowed. Rather, this rule invites us to see the intent behind the words. Doing so invokes people to act with positive intent.

This is not about persuasion or winning and losing; it is about listening and learning.

One example is the diversity, equity and inclusion (DEI) space. When discussing this area, we don't always know what words to use, and we're scared of causing offence or saying the wrong thing. We've scattered invisible eggshells that stop us from doing or saying anything.

What if we create a space where it is ok to try, even if we get it wrong? Sometimes we will say things that are offensive or ignorant, but how do we learn if we don't have space to try?

When I am looking for new words to describe something I'm wary of, I use the phrase, *'Extend me some grace, I'd like to ask something, but I don't know the correct words to use...'* Every time I do so, I am given the space to practice and I often get constructive feedback on my tone, language and framing.

This is not about persuasion or winning and losing; it is about listening and learning. Conversations enable us to learn and grow together, calibrating with each other and what we think is respectful and appropriate.

Culture is defined by all of us, by how we participate, and we are judged by the community we interact within. So, learning and growing together is essential to create a space where all feel welcome.

Try to hear what they're saying and see the good in it. You aren't rewriting what they're saying; you are listening with the intent to connect. They are human like you. We all have unique experiences that create our values frameworks.

No two humans have the same perspective of what is good, right and just in society. So whether you overlap in values a lot or a little, every person's framework has validity. That means embracing a compassionate response rather than an oppositional response.

My mantra here is 'judge less, love more'.

Listening is something we do with our ears, our minds, our hearts and our bodies. Body language is a signal of interest when listening. Like tone, if your conversation is cooling off or halted, it is likely because your body language is not open to receiving what others are sharing. What is the point of sharing if it seems you don't care?

The first LinkedIn article that said listening is nodding and saying bland confirming statements like 'Yep' created an unintended consequence. We now have an entire generation of people who believe active listening is acting like a bobblehead. Some people spend more energy trying to do activities labelled 'active listening' than actually listening.

Eye contact can build trust as eyes communicate intent regardless of what we say. Aim for a balanced amount of eye contact. There is a point where it is awkward, intense or too intimate if you maintain eye contact more than 70% of the time. The level of eye contact also depends on your relationships and culture and how much trust and connection already exists.

The environment is also a factor. When having conversations online or via video, we want to maintain connection and not looking at the camera can imply we are disinterested or distracted. There is a balance here because staring at a camera for hours is unsustainable.

Now, when listening deeply and intently, I sometimes look just to the side, upwards or down, to give my full attention to my ears and the words coming in. If I am doing this, I'll quickly offer a disclaimer like *'Hey I'm having trouble focusing right now, so I'm going to look just off to the side so I can really focus my senses on what you're saying. Is that alright with you?'* I sometimes wish it was acceptable to close my eyes and remove all visual distractions! That is one of the reasons I love a good phone conversation.

You can plan to use body language and eye contact to connect, but know that ultimately the most resonant variable is your intent. If you are not looking at the camera or person, they can tell if you are genuinely thinking through what they're saying, processing and responding. The opposite applies, too. If you are distractedly skimming your email or checking a notification, then abruptly jump back into the conversation, they will sense the disconnection.

Rather than getting wrapped up in the performance of listening, simply bring the intention to listen and stay with that intention.

Listen to what is unsaid. What is conveyed through the combination of words and language, other sounds or verbal cues in tone, silence and inflections and through the body and movement. All these inputs must be observed and taken on board when listening.

Deep listening requires a lot of practice and energy. I keep reminding myself to be aware of and to listen more deeply to the words and the meaning behind them. I'm right there with you, working on being a better listener.

Embracing wonder means listening through a lens of curiosity. When hearing what they're saying, notice what grabs your attention. What makes you want to ask follow-up questions? What words do they use that you find interesting? What snags your attention?

Take note of these as potential places to go in conversation. Whatever you find interesting will often lead to a conversation that everyone enjoys. It's how you get to common ground – they put something out there and you grab the pieces that resonate with you. Continuing to do this leads us to explore new frontiers together or go to new depths of a specific topic.

Listening goes wrong when you get wrapped up in your own reactions and thinking. Too often, I've had the awkward experience of being in my head when the other person stops talking. Did they ask a question? Did they simply pause? What do I say now?

If you do start to zone out, simply bring your awareness back and absorb the conversation from that point. You might miss some details, but at least you're with them again. It's also ok to say, *'Hey, I'm sorry, I was caught up thinking about what you said earlier. Would you mind repeating that last idea?'* Or even in that awkward silence, say, *'I'm sorry, I was thinking about your point, and was wondering about this aspect...'* followed by a question or a response.

Sometimes, they might be upset that you weren't listening and refuse to answer, which is a fair response. However, in my experience, the initial hurt of not being listened to is helped by admitting to this very common human fault, and then acknowledging you were considering something they said. They may even feel honoured that you thought about what they said, deeply or in a new way and feel excited to build the conversation from there.

Listening requires so much presence that I am still learning how to be with others in conversation, more than in my head. It's so easy to go off on a tangent or start thinking through a response. I want to sound smart and move things forward, so I spend time planning a response or framing a question instead of listening and letting my response flow out organically. It takes a mix of listening and identifying potential threads to respond and shape the conversation.

One tool to help with this is having a notebook or a piece of paper handy to jot quick keywords, questions or ideas. Paper and pen are less disruptive to connection than technology like a notes phone app or a laptop. With paper, they can see what I'm writing and that I'm still in the conversation with them. I also set the expectation with, *'Hey, I'm going to use my notebook in this meeting, not to take notes necessarily but to remember keywords and questions as we go through this conversation. It helps me focus.'* People are often worried or suspicious when someone is taking notes on their phone, so I try to alleviate their fears.

The conversation will be richer if you follow your curiosity. Adding energy and excitement to your follow-up is infectious, and the other participants will be swept along with you.

Respond

We can make small adjustments and change the fire completely. Shifting one log to prop up another opens a new pathway for oxygen to flow. Adding a log to cover a dwindling area can extinguish the flames or provide necessary fuel. Adjusting the chimney flue or air vents controls how much oxygen flows. Once the fire is going, you don't need much air. If there's too much oxygen, you'll burn through your firewood needlessly.

And when in doubt – wait. Be patient, and the fire will demonstrate what it needs. Sometimes, not messing around with it is the best course of action.

We open a conversation by asking, then listen and receive information. The final stage is your response. It is where you have the most opportunity to shape the conversation. You can prepare to some degree; however, it is probably the most complex aspect of conversations.

Responding is where it can get messy. It is volatile. A single response can lead to unexpected and beautiful places, completely disrupt the flow or even end the conversation abruptly. It has the potential to go in any direction.

Friction creates sparks. We could perceive this as negative, but we need sparks to light a fire. Rubbing up against one another ignites the fire within each of us. When combined with the intent to collaborate and define our shared culture, we come alive with co-creation.

We are most scared of volatility in conversation; the fear of creating a harmful interaction stops us from trying.

Yet, we have the power to guide conversations in directions that are uncomfortable and helpful. When we enter this complexity, we must recognise our bias for binary thinking — that situations are 'this' or 'that'.

Often we default our responses to being their idea or our idea, yes or no, black or white, when the best responses embrace the grey.

Responding in a way that honours both sides, using verbal tools like 'Yes, and...' allows us to explore the spaces between us without descending into oppositional arguments. It isn't us versus them; it's us working together towards the goal.

This stage is vital, so take your time. Use the power of the pause to consider your response. In my experience, people return the grace given in the listening aspect and will patiently wait for you to respond. Sometimes a response emerges, and at other times, you'll draw a blank. That's why I like to prepare a few stories, informational tidbits or questions, to have some ready

Use the power of the pause to consider your response.

Naturally, by talking things out and hearing other perspectives, we shift.

It is more powerful to gently provoke and invite new considerations and curiosity than to push and force someone into changing their beliefs.

---

responses. These give me time to percolate the new information and discover a new question or path.

This messy stage is where you will encounter disagreements. Be clear, though, that responding does not have to mean persuasion. That approach usually ends up in an oppositional battle, not an open and safe exchange of ideas. Rather than persuasion, consider encouragement, which is a gentler invitation.

It helps to loosen your grasp on your beliefs of what is right. If you hold tightly to your ideas, you're stuck in a binary with little space for new considerations or even to hear what the other person truly thinks.

Rather than engage in oppositional disagreements, wouldn't it be better to have a chat? To hear each other's perspectives and walk away — either confirming or questioning some aspects.

Whether we name it or not, every conversation changes us. Naturally, by talking things out and hearing other perspectives, we shift.

It is more powerful to gently provoke and invite new considerations and curiosity than to push and force someone into changing their beliefs. Has it ever worked for you? Do you blindly comply when someone tells you to do or think something? No, and I would bet you respond strongly in your defence. If that environment is created in a conversation, then everyone's walls go up. The safe, open space for exploration is lost and needs to be re-established.

Bringing generosity, love, openness and wonder – to **GLOW** – in our responses creates the most productive conversation. It's productive because it is a shared conversation with everyone participating and listening instead of shutting down and shouting.

When responding generously, build on what they have said. It might sound obvious, but sometimes we get distracted or want selfishly to drive the conversation in a particular direction.

What does going with the flow feel like? When you're really listening, you can hear what the person is trying to say and what they are trying to convey in their point through what is both said and what is not. Sometimes, I have to remember to be patient and go respectfully point-by-point to see it through.

Following the flow means responding with empathy or solutions. Empathetic responses would honour the emotions and give more space to air our feelings. Solutions are actions or practical things we can do in response to the situation. Sometimes I ask people what response they prefer, *'Would you like me to respond with empathy or actions?'* to clarify my role. Most of the time, it's empathy.

Let's say I'm chatting with my friend Dan. They're describing their workplace and how they're feeling pressured to work long hours. Following the flow would be asking about how it's impacting the rest of their life or listening to further explanations of the emotions. Not following the flow could be asking about something totally different, like their plans for the weekend.

Resist the urge to go on a tangent or skip to a new topic. If you do so, do it with intention. Facilitate the jump and explain why you want to, for example, *'I know we're talking about your workload, but I think it would be helpful if we jumped over to how the business is growing over the next six months because that will inform how your workload fits in. Is that ok with you? Is there anything you want to cover off before we hop over there?'*

Our intention is to grow the conversation. Generosity comes in because we want to build it so they can fully participate and honour all that has been shared.

Love takes our breath away. Disagreements do too. We often hold our breath unconsciously. The physiology of this is stark, and when you start to dial into your breath, you can instantly grasp whether you are in a space of fear or love.

Breath is the tool for finding our way back to responding with love. We can take a breath, refocus and align our intention before responding. Taking responsibility in that way is challenging but rewarding and results in a more positive experience for everyone involved.

Disagreements are often difficult and uncomfortable. They can be triggering and emotive and make us feel many big things at once. It can be overwhelming, and, at times, it is hard to maintain focus on the goal of the conversation. This responding stage is where we can assert control of the conversation.

Staying positive and kind is difficult, especially when the person you're chatting to is trying to bait you into fighting back.

Joel Levin is the founder and managing director of Aha! Consulting. He teaches perceptive strategies for dealing with opposition in community engagement,

Breath is the tool for finding our way back to responding with love.

with the phrase, 'Don't pick up the rope'.[9] When someone wants a fight, they will say things to provoke you. They want you to 'pick up the rope' and play tug-of-war until someone gives up or falls over. That outcome is dissatisfying, especially if the purpose of the conversation is to connect and find common ground.

Be aware of their intention and what their motivations are. Take the high road and diffuse the aggression. One tactic I used when talking to voters was to listen while they got all the heat out. Given space, anger starts as explosive and then gradually cools down. It's like a boiling kettle that keeps screaming, but if you open the valve and turn off the heat, it'll eventually run out of steam. This strategy takes a lot of patience and compassion but can be quite rewarding. After that emotional explosion, there is space for reflection, contemplation and exploration.

We always hope that a difficult conversation will resolve into a more meaningful shared dialogue, but they may choose to end it. If they continue, you get to engage in a golden conversation with respectful disagreement. If they don't, at least you didn't waste your time and energy on someone who is closed off.

Our response is always a choice to shape the tone of the conversation. We can choose to get into the mud, pick up the rope, get into a battle, and reduce

Our response is always a choice to shape the tone of the conversation.

the consciousness of our response and how we treat each other. The further down we get, the more our logical and social boundaries erode. We transform into wild creatures, acting only with the intent to harm or protect ourselves. It isn't a very conscious way of being.

We can instead choose love. By being aware of ourselves and our reactions, we find the spaciousness to choose an appropriate response. When we operate from a higher frequency, we are more conscious, more aware and more present to what is happening. We more easily respond with love.

This does not happen overnight, and sometimes, we still get triggered and become growling bears. But with practice, we continue to grow our capacity and more often can hold peace while in difficult conversations.

Choosing love as a response does not mean you are meek or weak. It is quite the opposite. You hold strength in your perspective and open up an avenue for exploration together.

That might sound like, *'I think recognising Pride Week is important for our queer colleagues. You mentioned that it segregates and highlights certain groups, which I get can feel unfair. How do you think we can better recognise every person's unique identity and life experience? What would feel fair from your perspective?'* In this example, you've shared your perspective and actively disagreed while opening a direction you both can relate to and discuss further.

In conversations, we want to unite and be positioned to explore the problem together, instead of acting as opposing forces. We can even explicitly say this to set an expectation of togetherness, which diffuses the tendency to take disagreement personally. If we are united and exploring the idea, question or problem together, everyone can participate fully without retribution and value each perspective.

When responding in a conversation, stories share information and experiences, which creates greater understanding and empathy. When you share something about yourself that is a bit raw or vulnerable, you subtly invite the other person to join you at that same level of honesty. It is very powerful to connect through shared experience.

Stories don't have to be deep to be meaningful. Imagine you're someone's boss; all they know about you is that you run meetings and hound them for deliverables. If they hear a story that is outside their perception of you, it creates a new connection. It humanises you. It could be a story of why you love kite surfing and reading the wind and waves. It could be how walking your dog is the highlight of your morning (pets and pictures of pets are like a cheat code for human connection). Maybe you read fantasy books because you like to escape to another world before you fall asleep. All these share a bit of who you are. They provide a thread for the other person to respond, with their own experience, *'I also read to escape!'* or with curiosity, *'I didn't realise you kite surf. Which beach is your go-to?'*. If they don't immediately know what to do with your story, you can ask, *'So what do you do for fun?'*.

To form a connection, we need to see each other as unique, messy, fallible, beautiful, different, and perfectly human. Not as roles or labels, the boxes we tick are confined within the walls of stereotypes and judgement.

Beware of selfish storytelling, where you share a story to highlight yourself or focus the conversation on you. Selfish storytelling is talking about yourself and your experience at every turn.

Have you ever had a conversation with someone who made it all about themselves? You could have shared that you're experiencing something horrible, and they respond with, *'That happened to me too…'* followed by five minutes of a rant. You don't feel heard or listened to when the response is selfish storytelling, because their stories are in service to themselves, not the shared conversation. Their mistake is that because they're sharing stories, they feel that's connecting, whereas what it does is devalue the story that was previously shared. It feels like they're piling on and centering the conversation around themselves. That is not the purpose of a conversation.

The purpose of stories is to create connection and share, *'Here is something about me'*, and for them to truly see you. When you extend a piece of yourself, most people respond in kind. It is an embedded and unspoken social contract.

To bring wonder into your response is to invite exaggerated and explicit exploration. You can set a frame that invites us to suspend reality and play within our imaginations. Reframing opens a new channel of exploration that doesn't have the baggage of our current situation.

This is where science fiction or allegories thrive — taking a concept and building a world to surround that one principle. It is absurd to consider any variable in a vacuum, yet by doing so we create a sandbox. Any idea is fair game; everyone can add whatever they like within the set parameters. More than ever, there are no wrong answers. This creates an environment where people participate without taking feedback personally because we're playing with ideas.

Sometimes, exaggerating a dimension can explain why we need to embrace the grey areas. Nothing is absolute. Everything plays within a shared context, interacting with everything around it. If the person you're chatting with sees the world as very black and white, this can be a helpful tool to help them recognise the necessity and presence of the grey area. To understand that two things can be true simultaneously. Each of us has a way of perceiving the world, which is neither right nor wrong.

Here are a few examples of reframing:

Exaggerate by time: *'Ok, so what if we took that idea and played it out 100 years into the future? What would that look like?'*

Exaggerate by value: *'What if we took the value of care and extended it throughout society by making care and care-based roles like child care the highest paid and highest valued? What would that be like?'*

Exaggerate by feeling: *'What if everyone did feel happy all the time? Would that be Utopia? Where would it go wrong? For example, what if your dog died and you felt happy?'*

There are infinite ways you can reframe with wonder. Over time, you'll develop preferences for how you like to direct conversations, much like my bias towards feelings and values.

These questions are fun because they separate us and our personal application from the idea or topic we're discussing. It is genuine play without consequences. This play gives us the creativity to imagine new and different possibilities.

While it might not seem productive, imagining new ways of being and doing creates a possible vision to build towards. Speaking it into being, like our ancestors have done for tens of thousands of years gathered around the fire.

Close

A fire can burn forever if there is fuel and oxygen. At some point, you'll need to decide to close it down and put it out.

When it's time to end, spreading the coals distributes the oxygen and fuel to meaningless levels, causing it to burn out quickly. If the fire is still burning, pour on water to extinguish it entirely.

Conversations are similar. The ask, listen and respond stages can interchange and continue for an infinite amount of time. That is why the facilitator needs to be intentional about closing the conversation.

Several times, I've asked a question and gone down a whole new path only to realise, a few minutes in, that I no longer have enough energy to listen and respond properly.

It is awkward and difficult to manage a quality conversation when it goes beyond attention limits (energy to listen and engage), curiosity or interest (far beyond things we care about), physical comfort (staying in a similar state for a prolonged period), or any other barriers to energy and intention.

It's the same for the participants. Most people are not practised at discussing their thoughts and feelings in a meaningful way, and playing at these depths takes energy. Be aware so you can close the conversation down before it becomes too taxing. If it's a bell curve of energy, aim to close between the 60%-80% mark so it ends with some engagement.

Build awareness of good exit points in a conversation. There is a cadence to conversations where it'll feel really buzzy and magnetic for periods and then naturally wane. Look for these signals of good moments to start closing the conversation.

More frequent and longer silence or pauses between voices. These little breaks could indicate a decline in energy or interest from the participants. It differs from a contemplative pause, where someone has stopped to consider. The tone of a contemplative pause still has electricity and energy — you can feel them working through it. A break that might indicate it's time to close is more like the exhale of breath, and you can choose whether to take in a new one and start again.

Repetition of ideas and statements that cannot be redirected. When you've reached an impasse and cannot divert in a new direction, then it's best to close and agree to disagree. You can always pick it up after everyone has gone away and reflected further.

Posture and body language are relatively clear indicators of how much energy and engagement people have. If people are leaning back in their chairs, slouching or have a melting vibe, you should probably close the conversation. That is different to the apathy or defiance you might get at the beginning of a conversation. At the end, they're almost empty, as if their bodies lack the life force to stay upright.

Closing can also create a chapter break. It doesn't have to mean the end of a conversation; many bigger topics need multiple conversations or chapters to fully explore and determine an outcome.

When facilitating a long day or a workshop, close the first 90 minutes with a stretch or a walk. Get people moving to create a natural break in the tension. Closing and taking a break or changing environments is a great way to reset a conversation.

The purpose of closing a conversation is to describe what should be remembered from this conversation, followed by any actions or next steps.

Conversations can flow in many directions, and this is your opportunity to curate the summary. Create a narrative highlighting the key messages we should all remember and share with others.

Your role is to name the common ground. Explicitly leave people there because our common ground is where love lies, with everyone feeling that golden, caramel tone of connection.

Before embarking on a big conversation, you can prepare a few different landing points. If you are truly in the conversation and listening intently, you will see the natural exit points, but sometimes you'll need to use a question or tool to indicate the conversation is nearing a close. Direct the conversation towards something that reviews what has been discussed and any outcomes or next steps.

When we close with generosity and love, we leave people feeling positive about our shared experience. Our openness permits everyone to be honest with their experience, and ultimately we go forth from this one-time conversation into greater reflection and action.

When recapping the conversation, be generous in how you represent everyone. The goal is for everyone to feel involved and that they contributed meaningfully. The generosity is in giving them recognition for their time, energy and sharing of self. Include a thank you and tone of gratitude in your close.

Highlight individual perspectives and, if needed, reframe their point to fit within common ground. By now, you should understand their view well enough to reframe it with integrity, not rewriting what they mean into something else.

For example, you might say, *'While we all agree that responsibility is essential to our jobs, we have some differences in how we demonstrate responsibility. Personally, I'm looking forward to reflecting on the different ways everyone interprets this word further. I hope we continue the conversation in a few weeks when we assess the project status.'*

A more specific call-out might sound like, *'Thank you all for the in-depth chat about what responsibility means in our work. I appreciate that we have differences in what this means. Sam thinks it's about the timeliness of showing up to meetings and returning documents, whereas Alex views it more like completing the task to the highest degree of quality regardless of timing. Both perspectives have value, and I hope that by becoming more aware of our unique approaches, we can leverage our strengths and work together better.'*

Everyone should feel accurately and positively represented.

It also doesn't have to be long. I was at a party recently and got into a 25-minute conversation with three other people. We talked about identity and how our ethnic or cultural backgrounds are embedded differently in our identity. Not a small topic for a chat at the pub, and each person went into the depths and shared honestly.

I wrapped it up by saying, *'I'm going to go and grab another drink, but I wanted to thank you all for sharing in such a rich discussion. Each of your stories has made me think a bit more about my own identity and orientation. How wonderful is that! Thank you again and enjoy continuing your own reflection!'* And off I went to the bar. That short wrap-up provided a bookend to a very meaningful interaction. Everyone left feeling acknowledged and connected.

The tone of how you leave a conversation is very important. You don't want people to feel frustrated or down on themselves. As far as possible, leave on a positive note. An easy way to do this is to describe what we agree on or what interests or feelings we share. Naming commonality makes us feel less alone, and that sense of connection creates a lovely golden feeling.

When we wrap our conversations, naming the common ground invokes love. We all share certain aspects of being human, whether we like it or not or whether we remember that part of ourselves. When we elevate our commonalities, we remind each other that we are all connected. And when we feel that connection to something far greater than ourselves, we cannot help but feel accepted and ultimately loved.

It also means giving each person a positive reflection of their contribution. Like, *'I really appreciate how you described that; I hadn't considered it that way'*, or *'Thanks for opening up and sharing your story; I have a much more empathic understanding of what it is like for you'*. This can be hard if they are difficult and disruptive, but if you look for the good, there is always something positive to elevate and reflect. Maybe that

---

Naming commonality makes us feel less alone, and that sense of connection creates a lovely golden feeling.

---

sounds like, *'Thanks for saying some things that are difficult to voice'*, or *'I see your passion for this topic'*.

Being positive doesn't mean ignoring the difficult bits. Be careful about leaving any aspects of the conversation unresolved, as this can create tension. When left to fester, these can create serious feelings or thoughts that take longer to resolve and heal. In difficult conversations, someone might feel outside — as if they are alone in their perspective. Bring them in as much as you can, knowing that, ultimately, you cannot control their experience.

If there are loose topic threads, name them and confirm they will not be resolved here and now. Without a resolution, some people might leave the conversation questioning or taking it personally. This can turn into frustration, sadness, self-loathing and various negative emotions.

Perhaps assign a next step for their resolution, such as having someone do more research or booking a follow-up conversation. Suggesting everyone go away and consider what was said is a possible next step. When we've considered something further, we often want to talk about it.

Sometimes there will be loose pieces. That is ok too, and by naming that reality you give everyone permission to let it be.

When we start a conversation, we lead with vulnerability, sharing an honest part of ourselves to demonstrate that it is safe. Closing is similar in that you can share your journey through the conversation, allowing others to feel their own experience.

Being open and honest in your assessment of the conversation and your experience adds integrity to the entire conversation. You might say, *'I felt awkward in the middle when we were talking about it, but that's ok because I'm glad we're having the chat'*. Or *'I didn't expect what you said, and I'm still processing it if I'm being honest'*.

This names the true emotions and experiences while reminding everyone that sharing and exploring together is the goal of a conversation. It is also where we can explicitly agree to disagree. Naming that reality releases any participant from a feeling of obligation or attachment to what was discussed.

You can say it simply as, *'Alas, I think we'll have to agree to disagree on this one!'*

Again, always aim for a gracious response. *'I think we have different perspectives. Thanks for sharing, so I could understand better where you're coming from.'*

A more nuanced version might sound like, *'I hear ya, and I think we simply have different perspectives. I try to remember that much of our world isn't binary black or white, right or wrong, and while we both believe we're right, the truth may be somewhere between our two perspectives.'*

It's ok, we're not likely to agree with everyone on everything. By explicitly stating this, we remember that we're all different. No two of us believe exactly the same about everything. Carbon copies exist when we get apathetic or give away our personal responsibility. Instead, we should be helping others to awaken and realise we all hold unique perspectives on any situation or topic.

As you close the conversation, leave everyone with a gift to take forward — something to keep pondering or an action to take. It isn't assigning work; it's showing what could be next. Humans are often reassured by knowing what is to come. Taking the mental load off and suggesting 'where to from here' eases, and often people will take the path of least resistance.

Of course, we must note tone here. You cannot offer people a path that is obviously beneficial solely to you. Such an imbalance rings hollow and many will distrust your motives for the entire conversation. It also cannot be by command or deception. You're aiming for a next step that is open and inclusive to all levels of participation, perspective and comfort.

My favourite next step is feeding everyone a final spark of curiosity: a wonder or a question for each person to continue contemplating. *'I wonder what it would be like if our team worked seamlessly utilising every person's strengths. What would that be like, and how would we get there? That's something I'll be considering.'* It builds on our shared conversation while providing substance for further reflection and analysis. It ensures that the content of the conversation continues to reverberate within each participant.

Another clear next step is encouraging everyone to continue the conversation. *'Thanks for the great conversation today. Continue the chat later with family, or with friends over the weekend, or with your teammates.'* The subtle suggestion to continue the conversation leaves people feeling excited and empowered, and this helps them get over the courage gap to start new and meaningful conversations.

Where To From Here

The tools in this book are offered to start you on the journey to golden conversations and greater connection. Reference it often for practical advice in sticky situations. It's your field guide. Mark it up, dog ear the pages and use it as you courageously lead and participate in fulfilling conversations.

I hope you facilitate a golden conversation for another. Once someone has experienced the magic, they know what is possible. They understand what level of connection we can achieve. They recognise how to navigate difference respectfully. When you model behaviour, you show others the way. You lead them to this shared heart space, our common ground.

In every conversation from now on, you are leading the way. Each conversation will shift and move people so they will go on to have meaningful conversations elsewhere. They will have seen what is possible and picked up new tools to use themselves.

Conversations change the world. You do so every time you open up and share a meaningful connection with someone.

Defining and exploring our common ground is essential for the progress of our society. Once we name our core values, we can stand by them and fight for them proudly as a united community. Hold each other mutually accountable and responsible for our shared culture.

We are in a crisis of leadership, where many people in traditional roles of power lack courage. The modern world has many complex, wicked problems which seem to go nowhere, so our collective trust in institutions is declining. At times, the system and all that is broken can feel overwhelming.

So, where do I find hope and inspiration?
With you.

We are all leaders. Every person, no matter their role, their neighbourhood, their skin colour or accent, has the power to lead in their own way, guiding others through invitation, not by force. By modelling, we show others the way.

Culture is shaped by participation. The actions we take every day ripple out and create culture change. Simply being is enough.

This is your work. This is my work. This is our work. By all of us, for all of us.

You are the firekeeper.

Instead of feeling anxious or bored with your conversations, you can prepare and bring new energy to any discussion. You know how to start and guide the fire, both intuitively as a human and now explicitly by understanding the Anatomy of Conversation.

Remember to open conversations with intention, dance through asking with curiosity, listen with care, respond with creativity, and, finally, to close with grace. Throughout your conversations, remember to simply **GLOW** – bring Generosity, Love, Openness and Wonder.

As our ancestors gathered, I offer this book as a fire of its own. A place to come for wisdom, inspiration and solidarity.

As you go forth courageously practising golden conversations, know you are not alone. Revisit the text, find a buddy to compare experiences with and reach out to me directly. I love having these conversations. Please join me as we learn together and forge a more connected and loving world.

About the Author

Emma activates leadership in change, one conversation at a time. She inspires people to take action and create inclusive change through speaking, training, conversations and strategic campaigns.

Emma's energetic, playful and dynamic approach enables everyone to participate and belong, creating change that sticks. She believes transformative change occurs through iteration, by walking together on common ground in a shared direction.

Emma has managed political and advocacy campaigns across the US and around the world for over 15 years, specialising in scaling grassroots movements. Her journey started in 2008, helping to elect Barack Obama, and she hasn't stopped believing in the power of people since.

Emma works with people and organisations to improve connection and courageous participation in culture change. Her offerings include keynotes for large groups, executive coaching, team workshops and in-depth culture change programs. To chat about your situation, please visit www.emmagibbens.com and book in a call.

As a daughter of a painter and a musician, you can often find Emma creating. She finds energy in creative play, whether it's playing cello, writing, painting, singing, poetry, or philosophy. Emma finds peace going on walks, looking at cool trees and gum nuts, and seeing the sun cast through the leaves.

Acknowledgements

This book is a testament to the collective wisdom that has been generously shared with me. Thank you to every person who I have ever shared a conversation with. My conversation craft has been honed through hundreds of insightful, intense, and awkward interactions with all kinds of people from all kinds of experiences. It is through interacting with you that I have come to know myself better, and I cannot thank you enough for that gift.

References

[1] Gladwell, M. (2008). *Outliers: The Story of Success*. New York: Back Bay Books.

[2] Myers, V. (n.d.). *Diversity and Inclusion*. [online] Available at: https://www.vernamyers.com/diversity-training/

[3] Oxford Dictionary. (2023). *Oxford Languages*. Oxford University Press.

[4] The On Being Project. (n.d.). *The Better Conversations Guide [online]* Available at https://onbeing.org/better-conversations-guide

[5] hooks, b. (2001). *all about love: new visions.* New York: Harper Perennial.

[6] Oxford Dictionary. (2023). *Oxford Languages.* Oxford University Press.

[7] Patterson, K., Grenny, J., Mcmillan, R. and Switzler, A. (2012). *Crucial Conversations: Tools for talking when stakes are high*. New York: McGraw-Hill.

[8] Perel, E. (2023). *Real Time with Bill Maher.* 21 April.

[9] Aha! Consulting. (n.d.). *Aha! Consulting | Engagement. Strategy. Facilitation. Training.* [online] Available at https://www.ahaconsulting.net.au

Questions to explore

Here is a place to add questions of your own! I've started you off with a few fun ones I use to build connection...

"What do you do for fun?"

"Which of the five senses (taste, touch, smell, sight and sound) is most useful and why?"

"What have you been curious about lately?"

"If you could wave a magic wand and change one thing in the world what would it be?"

Find more conversations and resources at
www.emmagibbens.com/conversation-starters

www.ingramcontent.com/pod-product-compliance
Lightning Source LLC
Chambersburg PA
CBHW052012030426
42334CB00029BA/3187

* 9 7 8 0 6 4 5 4 8 5 7 2 1 *